TERRIFIC TOYS

I0811266

TERRIFIC TOYS

# IN THE PAST

By William Anthony

KidHaven PUBLISHING

Published in 2025 by
KidHaven Publishing, an Imprint of Greenhaven Publishing, LLC
2544 Clinton St., Buffalo, NY 14224



**Written by:** William Anthony
**Edited by:** Madeline Tyler
**Designed by:** Danielle Webster-Jones

**Cataloging-in-Publication Data**

Names: Anthony, William.
Title: Terrific toys in the past / William Anthony.
Description: Buffalo, New York : KidHaven Publishing, 2025. | Series: Terrific toys |
Includes glossary and index.
Identifiers: ISBN 9781534547193 (pbk.) | ISBN 9781534547209 (library bound) | ISBN 9781534547216 (ebook)
Subjects: LCSH: Toys--Juvenile literature. | Toys--History--Juvenile literature.
Classification: LCC GV1218.5 A68 2025 | DDC 790.1'3309--dc23



Manufactured in the United States of America

CPSIA compliance information: Batch #CSKH25: For further information contact Greenhaven Publishing LLC at 1-844-317-7404.

Please visit our website, www.greenhavenpublishing.com.
For a free color catalog of all our high-quality books, call toll free 1-844-317-7404 or fax 1-844-317-7405.

Find us on

## Image Credits

All images are courtesy of Shutterstock.com, unless otherwise specified. With thanks to Getty Images, Thinkstock Photo and iStockphoto. Cover – StockPhotosArt, Vtldtlm, Phakorn Kasikij, kai keisuke, Shmelkova Nataliya. 4 – Yuganov Konstantin. 5 – Tracy Garbett. 6 – Prostock-studio. 7 – makalex69. 8 – HomeStudio, optimarc. 9 – Margo Harrison, Vjacheslav Shishlov. 10 – Peter Hummers [1] [CC BY-SA 2.0 (https://creativecommons.org/licenses/by-sa/2.0)], mstudeny. 11 – lobo235. 12 – Nataliia Dvukhimenna. 13 – British Library [CC0]. 14 – flowerino. 15 – WikiFido [CC BY-SA 4.0 (https://creativecommons.org/licenses/by-sa/4.0)]. 16 – Brookhaven National Laboratory (BNL) [Public domain]. 17 – Brian Kenney. 18 – oliveromg. 19 – Monkey Business Images. 20 – OnlyZoia, Hurst Photo, Robert Kneschke, Veja, Maria Spb, Ivonne Wierink. 21 – KerrysWorld, Tinxi, Brian Gallegos, Housing Works Thrift Shops. 22 – JuliaGrin, SerbBgd. 23 – chinahbzyg, stacyarturogi, intoit.

# Contents



Words that look like this can be found in the glossary on page 24.

# Toys Long Ago

Toys are amazing! They're fun to play with and you can learn lots with them. Children just like you have been playing with toys for thousands of years.

What is your favorite toy?

Over 5,000 years ago, ancient Egyptian children played with stone marbles.

Over 2,000 years ago, Greek children played with yo-yos and made dolls using **clay**.

Just like yo-yos, many other toys from thousands of years ago are still played with today!

# Teddy Bears and Dolls

Do you have a teddy? What is its name?

Teddy bears are named after an American **president** called Theodore Roosevelt. President Roosevelt's **nickname** was Teddy. Teddy bears were first made in 1902.

Dolls have been played with for thousands of years. In the past, dolls were made from all sorts of things. Children had dolls made from clay, wood, and even stone.

Today, dolls are normally made from plastic.

# Tudor and Victorian Toys

Children in Tudor Britain played with toys that were much simpler than the ones we have today. A Tudor toy box may have included wooden spinning tops and a cup and ball.

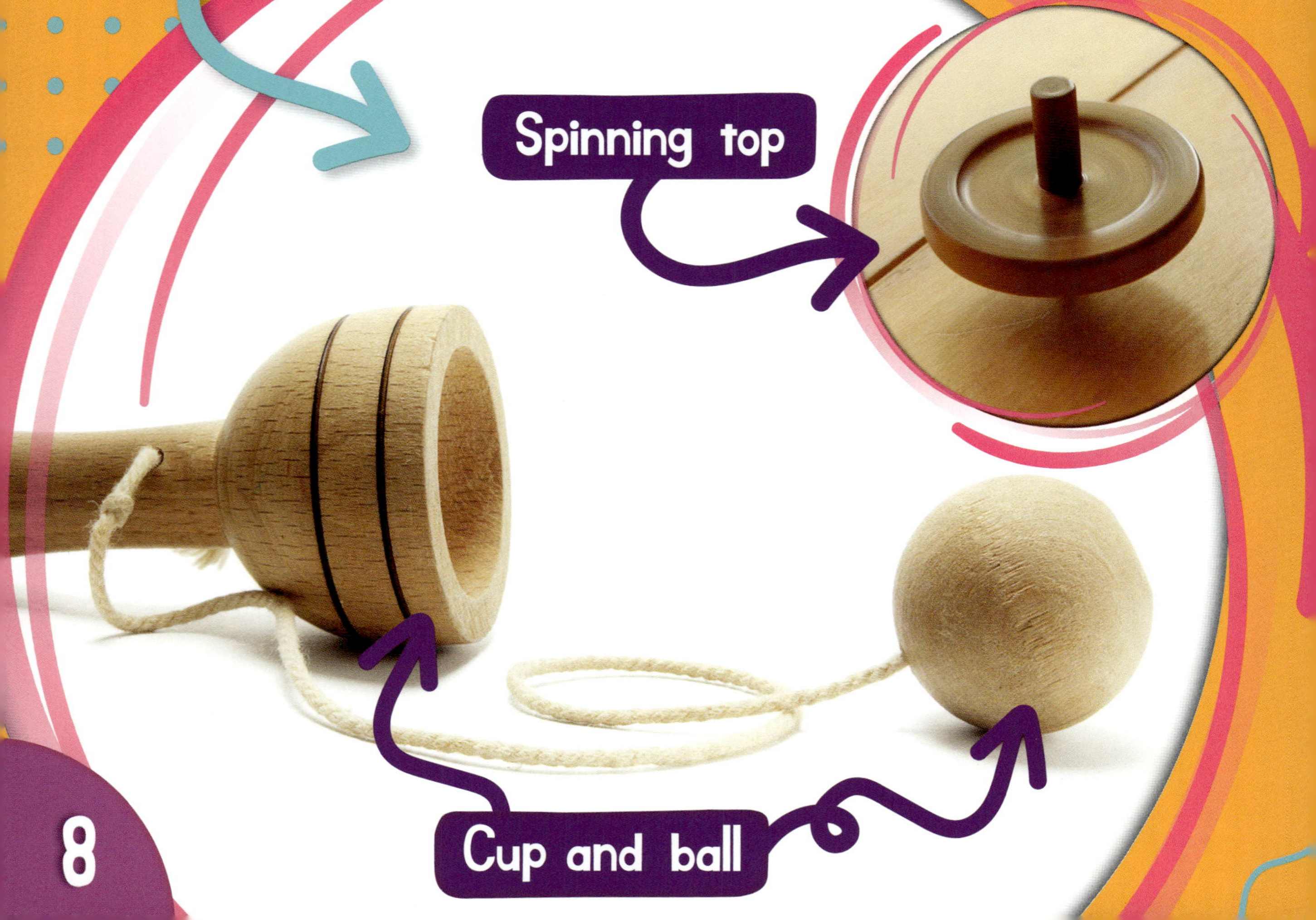

Children in the past didn't have computers or tablets to play games on.

Children in **Victorian** Britain played with big dollhouses and rocking horses.

# Playing Outside

The scooter is a toy made for children to get around outside. People attached the wheels from roller skates to a plank of wood with some kind of handle.

Scooter

**Have you ever tried to make your own toy?**

Pogo sticks were invented over 100 years ago. They are used by standing on the footrests and bouncing on a large spring. Pogo sticks are still used today.

# Puzzles and Games

Puzzles and games are fun because they can be very challenging. A game called Go dates back to around 4,000 years ago in China. A player must try to surround all the other player's pieces.

Jigsaw puzzles are pictures that you must put together from oddly shaped pieces that fit together. The first jigsaw puzzle was made over 250 years ago.

The first jigsaw puzzle was a map of the world.

What is the biggest jigsaw puzzle you've ever finished?

# Collecting

Lots of people collect old toys. Some people do it as a hobby. Old dolls are a common toy that people might collect.

Milk caps, also called Pogs, were part of a very popular game in the 1990s. They became part of a craze and many people collected lots of caps.

Do you have any collections of old toys?

Milk caps

# Video Games

The video games you play today are very different from the video games of the past. One of the first video games was called Tennis for Two. It was invented in 1958.

Tennis for Two was played by hitting a ball back and forth on a screen until one player missed.

Tennis for Two

Arcade

As technology got better and better, people were able to visit places called arcades to play their favorite video games.

# Toys for Girls and Boys?

In the past, many people thought girls and boys should play with different toys. Some people thought girls should play with dolls and boys should play with cars.

Why do you think people thought this?

We all know that every toy is fun for both boys and girls. Anyone can play with any toy, because every toy is great!

# Toys Through Time

1860s

The first toy trains were invented.

1919

The pogo stick was invented.

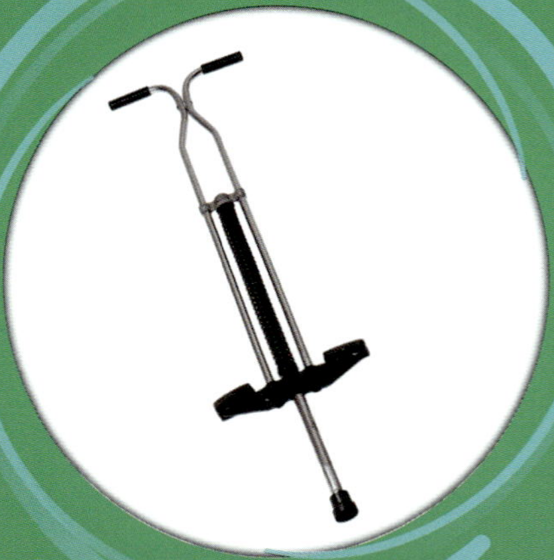

1949

Lego bricks went on sale.

1957

The Frisbee was invented.

1959

Barbie went on sale.

## 1960s

Twister and Operation went on sale.

## 1970s

Video game consoles became popular.

## 1980s

Nintendo's first console went on sale.

## 1990s

Roller skates and Beanie Babies were crazes.

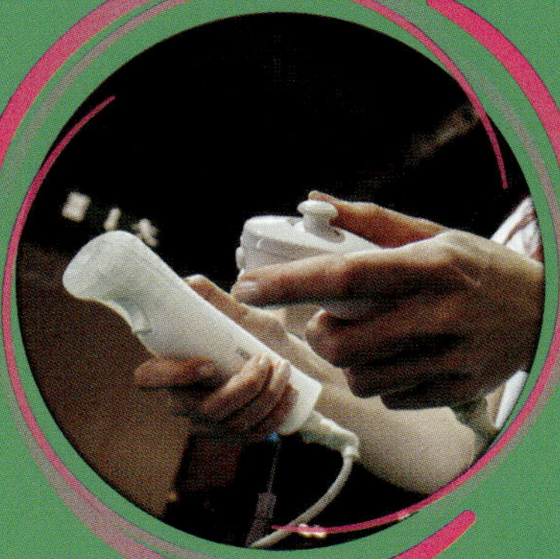

## 2006

Nintendo Wii games console was launched.

# Fun Facts

Barbie's full name is Barbara Millicent Roberts.

Play-Doh was never meant to be a toy. It was first invented to clean wallpaper.

Kites are thought to have been invented in China over 2,000 years ago.

The doll and the yo-yo are thought to be the oldest toys in the world.

# Glossary

| | |
|---|---|
| **challenging** | difficult in a way that is usually interesting or enjoyable |
| **clay** | a heavy, sticky material from the earth that can be made into different shapes |
| **craze** | something that is very popular for a period of time |
| **delicate** | easily broken or damaged |
| **nickname** | a name that is different from your real name, but is what your family or friends may call you |
| **president** | the person in charge of the government in some countries |
| **surround** | to be on or around every side of something |
| **Tudor** | relating to the period of British history from 1485 to 1603 |
| **Victorian** | relating to the period from 1837 to 1901 when Queen Victoria ruled England |

# Index